Body As Landscape

An Anthology of Prairie Beings

Fishtrap Outpost on the Zumwalt Prairie 2024
With CMarie Fuhrman
Edited by Francis Opila, Connie Wieneke, & Tom Butts

ISBN-13: 978-1-965492-07-9

Edited by Francis Opila, Connie Wieneke, & Tom Butts
Book Design by A.B. Hale
Cover Design by A.B. Hale

Published by
Blue Feathered Quill
Evans, Colorado, USA

Blue Feathered Quill | Trade Paperback Edition | June 2025

Body As Landscape

PHOTOGRAPHY BY:
Francis Opila
Connie Wieneke
Amelia Díaz Ettinger
Carol Dodds
Tom Butts
CMarie Fuhrman

ILLUSTRATIONS BY:
Janet Hohmann

CONTENTS

FOREWORD

Imagine with me, if you will.

A prairie. Tall grass and flowers. Wind sometimes. Rain, too. It undulates and for moments it seems that the thin veil of time is lifted. The cairns that have stood looking over this landscape for hundreds of years are fresh in the making. The footprints of the maker still warm. The veil not only lifts between past, present, and future, but between species. Listening, you hear the land speak. You can translate the song of coyote. You understand the deep whispers, those beneath the bark of the pine. Listening, you hear voices future and past. You hear songs and verse and prose and wonder.

The stories and poems in this collection are what you might hear. The words uttered silently or sung to a backdrop of flute are the words that a community of deeply caring, deeply listening humans were inspired to make. Were inspired to share. Are offering to you, should you lay your ear to the pages, give your eyes to their ideas.

Among the great honors of my life, is the opportunity to spend a week in community with humans and other beings on the glorious, majestic, and in some ways tragic Zumwalt Prairie. Every year, I learn something new about this place, the people in it, both present and past, and the future that many wish to steward the prairie into, a return to a more natural state of being. Companioned by my friend Janet Hohmann, a biologist and naturalist, we watch as these writers, detached from technology, also return to a more natural state of being and connect with the land and with one another.

Just as the prairie offers hundreds of different ways of knowing life, each of these writers offers a different way of seeing and being in place. Whether chirping with laughter, howling with sadness, or simply swaying in beauty, each writer is offering you something of the prairie and themselves, and in doing so, reflecting your own nature and beauty back to you.

This is the magic of lifting the veil. What it exposes is that we—landscape, time, species, communities—are all connected, and that to tell one story is to create another, to sing one song is to honor another. Let this collection be a talisman against despair, a guidebook into the greater than human, a message for the future, and an honoring of the past. You are in good hands here. You are standing in deep grasses; you are looking over grand vistas into deep gorges. You are listening and what you hear is life.

CMarie Fuhrman
McCall, ID
November 11, 2024

BIRDS OBSERVED

These are the birds we observed during our stay at the Zumwalt Prairie Reserve, including at Buckhorn Lookout.

Compiled by Tom Butts and Janet Hohmann

Killdeer
Wilson's snipe
Mallard
Cinnamon teal
Northern pintail
Canada goose
American kestrel
Ferruginous hawk
Red-tailed hawk
Swainson's hawk
Cooper's hawk
Golden eagle
Great-horned owl
Black-billed magpie
American crow
Common raven
Red-winged blackbird
Brewer's blackbird
Common nighthawk
Lewis's woodpecker
Hairy woodpecker

Northern flicker
Cliff swallow
Tree swallow
Barn swallow
American robin
Mountain bluebird
Western tanager
Western wood pewee
Spotted towhee
House wren
Townsend's warbler
Dark-eyed junco
Vesper sparrow
Song sparrow
Grasshopper sparrow
Chipping sparrow
Western meadowlark
Horned lark
Pine Siskin
American goldfinch
European starling

Wildflowers Observed

These are some of the wildflowers we observed during our stay at the Zumwalt Prairie Reserve, including at Buckhorn Lookout.
Compiled by Janet Hohmann

White Blooming
Yarrow
Slender pussytoes
Creamy buckwheat
Scarlet gilia (white form)
Elk thistle
Chickweed
Death camas
Prairie star
Mariposa (Sego) lily
Wild onion
False solomon's seal
False hellebore
Wild strawberry
Bladder campion
Eyelash weed
Monument plant (Green gentian)
Coral bells (Heuchera)

CLARKIA
JH '24

Janet Hohmann

Pink/Red Blooming
Clarkia (Elkhorn)
Sticky geranium
Scarlet gilia
Western dock
Big-head clover
Collomia
Filaree (Storksbill)
Wild hollyhock
Red columbine
Prairie smoke
Wild rose
Marsh paintbrush
Owl clover
Showy phlox

STICKY GERANIUM
JH '24

Janet Hohmann

3

Yellow Blooming
Arrowleaf balsamroot
Hoary balsamroot
Oregon grape
Sulfur buckwheat
Stonecrop (Sedum)
Tumble mustard
Smooth violet
Oregon sunshine
Sawtooth senecio (Groundsel)
Gray's desert parsley
Cous desert parsley
Cinquefoil (Potentilla)
Pale wallowa paintbrush
Western monkeyflower
Common puccoon
Wooly mullein
Wormwood artemisia
Gumweed
False dandelion
Goatsbeard
Arnica (various kinds)
Fiddleneck

Mariposa (Sego) Lily—Connie Wieneke

Blue/Purple Blooming
Brodeia (Blue dicks)
Common camas
Shining gentian
Lupine
Long-spurred violet
Larkspur
Horsemint
Skullcap
Blue-eyed mary
Shrubby penstemon
Taper-leaved penstemon
Bluebells
Blue stickseed
Teasel
Purple fleabane
Chicory

JANIE TIPPETT

In my former life I was a Bluebird

If you look into my eyes, you will see blue feathers.

What you can't see: my soul where a small Bluebird dwells. Its heart beats with mine, and as I age, its blood becomes visible in my eyes, eyes that have seen many seasons come and go, many changes in our world. Despite the passage of time, landscapes and cultures, there is still "Hope," Emily Dickinson's "thing with feathers," the thing I have become.

On the windowsill above my kitchen sink a small blown glass Bluebird perches, brilliant in the morning sunlight. She reminds me of my former life*. A free life, winging over high grassy ridges, hunting insects, feeling the Prairie breezes, catching wind currents, experiencing joy in my youthful body, falling in love, flying with my mate, building a nest, raising a family on the high moraine of Wallowa Lake. I lived out my short life surrounded by beauty, buffeted by storms, flew southward in Winter, and returned in Spring.

There were sad times: children eaten by hawks and other predators. All in all a good life. At the end: I was born again in Janie's soul.

From birth, my mother sensed I was different. My blue eyes always staring off somewhere in the sky, always searching. When I began to toddle around, I was attracted to birds, and poppies, Johnny-Jump-Up's, bluebells, all the colorful *wildings* that grew in the Sierra Foothills of my youth. My mother saw to it that I was exposed to beauty at an early age. I was left for hours outside in our backyard, happily waving my arms or napping in my buggy—alone, with butterflies, clouds, blue sky, and bird song.

I remember experiencing my first Bluebird. It was like watching a fragment of blue sky flutter hither and yon. I was fascinated and charmed by its color. I laughed, bringing joy to all who beheld me, which pleased my mother.

As I come to the end of another life, I wonder where my Bluebird soul will fly next? I like to think it will be free out here on this Prairie, here where I write in the midst of one of the last wild places. I like to think my soul will glide over the vastness of this Prairie, its rolling hills, tiny creeks, rock outcroppings, and acres of open sky, and joy to all who behold me. And my ageless soul will live again, my heart will beat with Dickinson: "Hope is the thing with feathers."

---

*   I realized after writing this that it is the male Bluebird that is bright blue, not the female. Oh well, souls are colorless, right?

Early Morning Musings

What's left of June's Pink Full Moon hangs in the early morning sky, but 'tis the color of white cloud and the only cloud in this perfect Summer sky.

I am perched on a lichen-covered rock that overlooks a landscape that fits my body, a body that is, at this moment, as much a part of the landscape as the rock I'm sitting on. The same fresh, soft breathing breeze that rustles the native bunch grasses, loosens tendrils of my white hair. If I sit perfectly still, I feel absorbed into the great silence of this high wild plateau. Little has changed since the Nez Perce roamed here for eons.

Perhaps an aging Nez Perce woman sat on this same rock. Knowing she didn't have pen and paper, she nonetheless must have contemplated growing older. She must've sensed, as do I, the companionship of this wild place, felt this same morning breeze, breathed deeply scents of pink geranium and sage, sensed the seasonal shift, observed the remnants of Spring lingering among the maturing grasses, listened to the trickling of the creek and how its flow is diminishing, heard the baby meadowlarks find their voices. She probably sang the Prairie song, knowing she, too, was the Prairie, just as she was the coyote, the owl, simply another aging rock.

When we live in a place we love, really LOVE, we become part of it. I know it to be true, and when I die, I won't die. My song will still be sung, just as sure as the June moon will ride the skies, the Prairie Smoke will drift away and reappear next Spring. Our seeds will drift and co-mingle with the wind, then seek some fertile plot of soil to sprout again.

As I write 'midst this wild Prairie, write about its vast silences, I contemplate these things. The sun has gone from warm to hot. Its intensity speaks to me. I strip down to my bra. Oh! The joy! I have a conversation with a bee, about pollination, about propagating beauty, and put a period to this jumble of words.

I have no watch, no cell phone, only know my stomach is rumbling with hunger. Soon the breakfast triangle will jingle jangle, and I have a steep hill to descend to rejoin my pack. Suddenly, I remember, and chin to sky, I raise my voice and chin to sky, and let loose a howl before beginning the rocky trail to breakfast. And then I hear my answer: many wild voices, a long drawn-out howl.

Breakfast is ready. I smile. My pack must have made a kill.

The Body As Landscape

On midsummer days I am reminded of a long ago hot August afternoon, when I hiked a steep trail into the Wallowa Wilderness to Slick Rock, a series of waterfalls that cascade over high rock terraces and into numerous pools. These snowmelt pools pause long enough on hot sunny rocks to warm themselves.

The sun-warmed pools continue to slip over the solid rock face in a lovely fashion and form tiny bathtubs that invite anyone to bathe, especially souls like me, souls with their wild side. My Bluebird soul is drawn here to such places.

I make my sweaty way up and up that hot August trail. Leaving my earthly skin behind, I dream of this place I've been many times before. I can already feel the water cascading through my hair, kissing my up-turned face, baptizing me. When I immerse myself in *this* wild place—like all wild places—there is so much beauty, it hurts.

At a favorite pool, I shed my human clothes and become Animal. I love my naked body, and melt into my surroundings, breathing in the water scent, a scent mixed with the mint that trembles from rock crevices. I shudder beneath falling mists, warmed by rock, and run my hands over my body, gasping, as snowmelt water touches my bare skin…

…*back at home, I step into my shower, and see white walls, a soap shelf, the small hose connected to a water source. I spray my hair and body, soap up and spray to rinse…*

…and after a time, here at Slick Rock, I wash my hair, without soap—the water, so soft, I don't need any. I feel warm, then cold, as pooling water spills over to the next level…water, born in beauty. Above me, tower massive talus slopes. Within their depths, seeping rivulets of snowmelt trickle forth to join the streams dashing downward.

Far below I hear Hurricane Creek as it falls into the large foaming pool I cannot see, but I know it is there, and above the creek rears the highest peak in the Wallowas, Sacajawea. I soak in the sight of her granite and basalt ramparts, her melting snows, her eroding sides. Her summit kisses a turquoise sky.

Suddenly, my body is alive! Alive to all the senses. Years are shed and I am 16 again. A cluster of purple penstemon springs from a rock outcropping. I smile. The sun smiles. My body is transformed. I feel part of the landscape.

A swallowtail butterfly nectars the shivering penstemons. A tiny Bluebird sips water at the edge of the pool, allowing the spray to soak its tiny feathers, and as I watch it bathe, suddenly, I am that Bluebird. I lie on my back, immersing myself, even further, into my surroundings. Water pools in my navel, spills over and into ferny places, trickles into tiny crevices, and back onto rock. Warmed by my body, the water flows on. I contemplate the mingling of our waters: snowmelt, Bluebird, and mine.

Here, we all breathe the same air, absorb the same water, speak the same language… 'midst the beauty that bruises our very Souls. Our Skins wear down, until, at last, we ALL return to stardust.

Amelia Díaz Ettinger

AMELIA DÍAZ ETTINGER

Zumwalt Prairie,

you'll let the world
soften you with its touch—Ruth Awad, "Reasons to Live"

where in my body can i hold you?
a place of grama and endless sky
what rock, insect, or cloud do i narrate?
in your space i'm frightened
do i pine for the comfort of my forest?
where the pileated drilled the core of a larch
just the other day

this lack of conifers
robs me of solace
in the exposure of a blistered
boulder covered in lichen
lovely but foreign

your lupine is left to dry alone
under a murderous sun
while arid crickets rumble
on grasses that abound

your landscape wants
to grow within me
a reminder that i can walk
in this world or engulf it

so, i'll lay myself bare on you
my skin, after all, is the color
of your soil
and like you, not quite yet infertile

i'll promise to step lightly
only on your trampled paths
that remind me of the others
that came before me and tended you

Zumwalt Prairie Home

here, the sky is male
a laceration of blue

this is the want of the prairie
her call to lay bare under his eye

there are no secrets for them
in this home without secluded shelters

even the badgers' dens
lose confidence in this exposure

of constant sun and furious winds
and rapid-running creatures

and still, if you peer
a little closer you also hear

the Tree Swallows'
sweeping conversations

in and out of cavities movement set
with the Horned Larks' two-note song

there's a beacon unabashed
with the Golden-mantled

Squirrels who entice
the Swainson's Hawk

this is not the quiet home you see
upon arrival on its open space

here is a feast, a smorgasbord
of wants struggles and successes

raven coyote and cloud
wailing even late into the night

where a living sky of stars
sashes the quiet view of grass

Cumulus

i never knew that what i saw
was my shape my shadow

nor do i remember
when the sky invented me

from the sea vapor
as i rolled over land without lips

couldn't savor trees nor dirt
no hands to touch this *herenow*

i worry why i slid over mountains
why everything i saw was drab

it wasn't until i finally ebbed
as rain over a river—

when my shape
no longer cruised overland

that i understood
that it was me all along

with my back
against

the vastness of sunlight

CAROL DODDS

Orison

The rush of wind down canyon
The perfect cleanse release
Negative perspectives move
To find a place of peace

Re - cognizing
Re - connoitering
Re - conditioning
Toward the balance point

Find common ground like the green ridge
Re - covering the wicked burn
Wipe away the prejudice I see too late

Less force - more kindness
Less absolute - more grace
Less agro - more honey
Help to find the perfect space

Think twice - speak once
Hear your thought-then fight
Reflect within - re - cover
Hurt re-judged made less a slight

First, I must find
The yin in the yang
The plus in the minus
The love in the hate

All come together in the end
Ah-men!

Carol Dodds

First Night

Snuggled into the blanketed cocoon, the hood taut around my face
I watch for the sun to take her final bow and leave the ridge
Impatient for the stars to pop out of an ebony pitch
I coax distant revelations while the moon circles

Please stay awake to savor stardom!   O joy!

Shooting stars, a satellite, winkers, new designs
Is this the same sky? …   ahh, Prairie sky
My face keeps starlight warm
Drifting into celestial dream

Morning enroute … horizon gentle hues
While sun announces off the telltale moon
The most gentle frost covers me…Dare I call it frost-dew not wet
The moon argues with the sun for her lag time
Thankful life - the day blossoms

Sneaking out, I try not to waken the frigid grass
I head out to welcome the hidden sun
My breath was solo at awakening
but at the fence I can see it flowing before me
The frosty joy tickles

Need to go quietly up past the barn while others sleep
I don't get past the bridge
A tiny spit of water over the rocks reflects the sky's greeting
Delicate reeds revel in the water
in celebration of the day

Tiptoeing up the rocky road
I find verdure to grace my steps with quietness
And reach skyward arms outstretched to encourage the day
Nearby tiny basalt columns rise in concert while some veer off at angles
The sun will love this face

I glance back toward camp
The concave draw nestled between variegated carpet hills
undulates in morning breath
Soon the light sauna will bring it back to balance

Anatomy

I AM the prairie
The prairie IS me
Despite the surround
Looking straight through WE

Down to the bedrock
Thin soil skin grips all
Generations' deep knowledge
Blossom and fall

Wind carries the message
Fire - the mess\age
Time - past with present
Leave no mark at pass\age

Ancient rocks represent life gone by
Forever and always directions to try
I cannot tell you, for I do not know
Ancestors witness but do not show

Who knows the future?
Or deep in the past?
The prairies will tell you
If you only ask

Comfortable rolling hills my form
Mimicking my eons-old mud norm

Age brings fresh freedom
Concern blows away
Prairie as monument
Stalwart for today

CONNIE WIENEKE

Today's Soul Map

Here, one map of Soul: this on-my-knees,
belly-up, heart-sundering before Prairie,
before a cataclysm of light. Here, the road
I left is realigned each dawn. Here, come
evening, a re-baptismal font. Instead of a
Priest finger-crossing my forehead, now
hands of strangers—left and right,
sacral community—ordain. Instead of
the Word that once held, my breath turns
to words—faces facing the setting sun—
to ash within one last bright bright circle.

Here, each morning I awaken, *neti neti**, slower
even than this or that, and rise with the falling
notes—call it today—snipe

        snipe

                snipe

and just there, such carrying-on by red-winged
blackbirds and one raucous duck—don't ask her
name—that one so alarmed her rapid rush—
makes me gasp. What are they all trying to say,
at what do they hint? Could it be: *Come hither
to this small stream?* or *Stay clear of this place
where I feed?* Today I call it: Song Letting Loose.

                Here, what I like
to call my sanctuary is as brief as an eye blinks,
as quickly gone as my breath comes-in goes-out.
Here, I am twisted&turned by north&west winds—
their hellos&fare-thee-wells followed by another
hola-y-hasta la vista. I am swept up by bunch-
grass—more holy than touch—swish_swish_
swish. The future—call it pollen—settles my skin,
bows my shoulders, the poles of my tent, slips
seeds between my ribs, breaks what I thought
might protect. I call it both blessing and bane.
More likely it's nothing more than my—yours, too?

---

*   *neti neti* in Sanskrit, means, among other things, "not this, not that."

—indefatigable naming of all I think I see&hear,
taste&smell, feel—   while all the while
a ferruginous hawk takes little notice.   Still
I have come to believe the lapis lazuli winged
and the quivering aspen light   do listen.

With night's slow drumroll fall, out of the dark
Flute lifts a bit of—call it if you must—veil, hope,
fear—or perhaps it is nothing but the rustling
of a gopher under my tent. Such night music
dispels what's between us and this earth, Earth
the only name we need for abundance. Isn't
Earth the only name for all we stand to lose?

But then!   Coyotes!
chorus the moon to rise so we can sleep. Coyotes!
nudge us to remember we are Nothing if not this dust
between our toes and the stars we try to push off.

Connie Wieneke

Francis Opila

First Morning on the Prairie

1 Waking

My own personal meadowlark
wakes me before sunrise
its gurgling song descends
        into liquid notes
                that drip onto bunchgrass.
A Belding's ground squirrel scampers
        up a wooden fence post,
inspects our world, regards
        the morning moon in the west
as it sets over the grounded
                grassy knoll.

2 Western Meadowlark Sings to Me

Wake up
lie there in your blueness for a moment
but   *Wake up*   *Wake up*
                to oceans of harmonies
of bunchgrass, butterflies, and gnats.
Watch the white hawk fly over you—
        the sky-being you came to see.
Follow him into clear blue
        drift in any direction you're drawn.
Then feel your feet on Earth.
Give thanks that you walk on Her,
that even if you fall
                you are still held.

3 After Waking

I didn't see my meadowlark fly away
but now I truly behold
        blue of sky.

Where Boundaries Dwell

Ekphrastic poem in response to The Nature Conservancy's
Zumwalt Prairie Preserve map

Yes, let there be lines
like ridges or rivers
or property bounds—
but mostly I prefer colors
chartreuse, magenta, canary, lapis
bunchgrass, wildflowers & sky
       spirals of silver
       green tea leaves
              that steep in oceans of prairie.

Tell me
       where we are now—
somewhere in the blazing sun
       on the Zumwalt
lupine sings lavender
swallowtails float yellow & scatter
howls of coyotes carry
       across contours & fences
the white Ferruginous hawk
       threads through azure skies.

Tell me
       where do our boundaries
       fall, shift & drift?

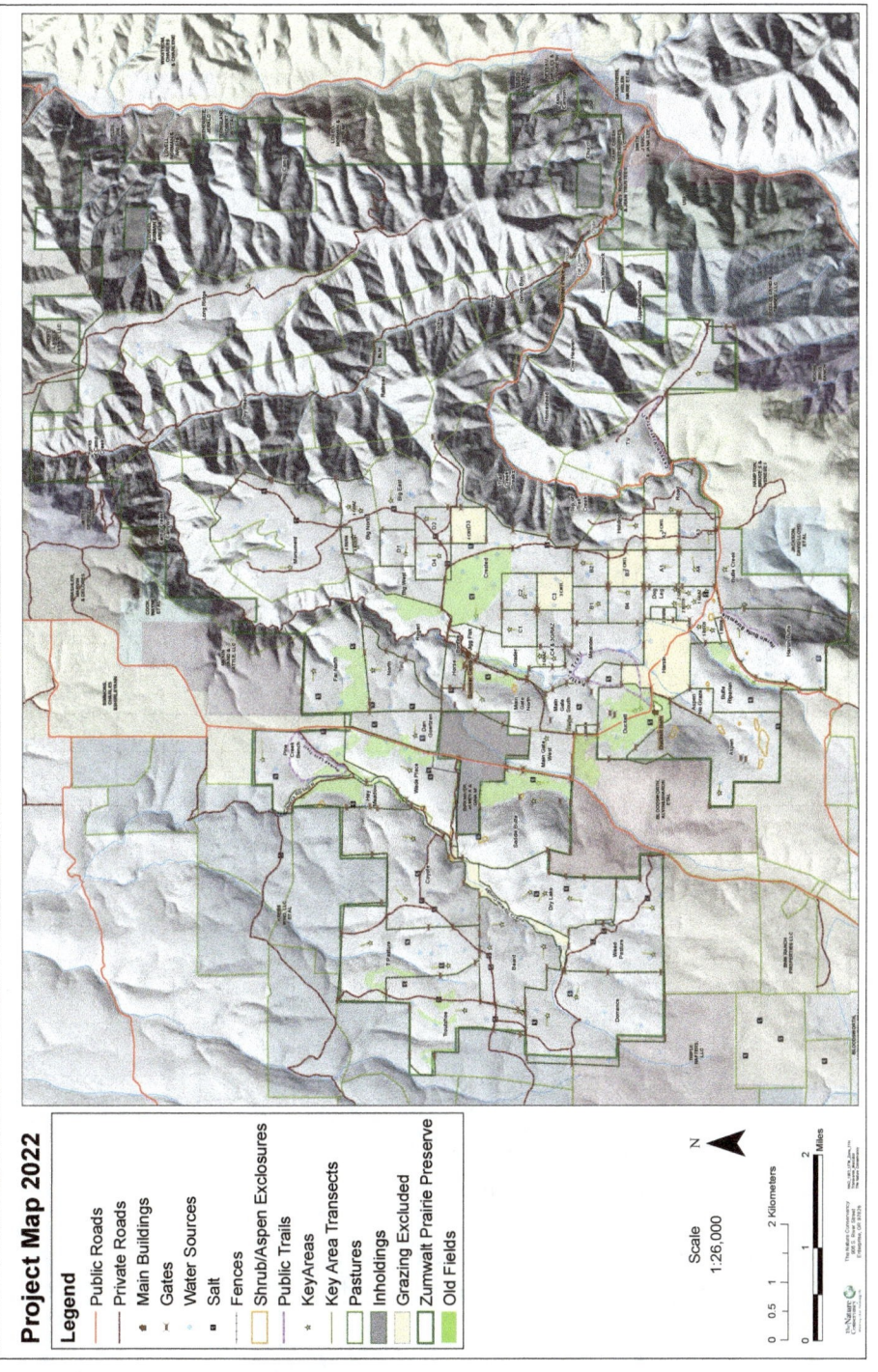

Zumwalt Prairie Map—The Nature Conservancy

Zumwalt Prairie Ghazal

Over wild grass, mule deer & elk graze on the prairie
Time morphs, nights become days on the prairie

Lupine, penstemon, prairie smoke & bees
bunchgrass—all woven in braids on the prairie

Listen to songs of meadowlark, gusts of wind,
frolic of squirrels in their maze on the prairie

Nighthawks swoop & dive, snipes winnow
up high, fading sunlight's ablaze on the prairie

Tell me, wind spirit, is this where I find solace?
On this open ridge my poem prays on the prairie

Adrift wanderer, how do you find your way
when wildfires in you blaze on the prairie?

Rockjacks hold fences steady in wind & sleet
What you whisper here stays on the prairie

We gather round the basalt cairn, inhale scents
of wild rose, fall into ecstatic craze on the prairie

My mind wanders like wind down a knoll
A sea of grass swells and sways on the prairie

Visions of *Nimiipuu** shimmer in the night sky
At moonrise, coyotes howl in praise of the prairie

Watch the star gods dance in black night
Only an errant soul betrays the prairie

My lost love flies by like the great white hawk
In blue sky she soars a long ways on the prairie

At nightfall Francis invokes the hollow cedar flute
An ancient voice lifts, warbles & graces the prairie

---

*   people of the Nez Perce tribe

22

Prairie Smoke flowers—Francis Opila

Prairie Smoke fruit—Francis Opila

Janie's Garden with Kelly—Francis Opila

REBECCA E. WILLIAMS
What Kind of Magpie

Janie has a soft-focus tuft of white around her mottled and high forehead and the skin of her cheeks is long from the long pull of the earth on them. Janie shows me her garden, her handy work at growing in the soft pebbling black dirt that has rolled off the mountains these past 10,000 years. Janie uses cattlebones as row markers— which leech their many minerals into the dirt, she says, they help the plants to grow. In Janie's garden, vegetables eat bones that stick up out of the ground like strange scoops, like weathered headstones. I bent down among her beets and pulled the fine-eared-red-veined leaves of unwanted amaranth until they were uprooted. I set their already wilting corpses to decompose alongside the living beets they were poised to overtake, whose roots would soon coalesce into a red and sweet heart so swollen it would burst through the soil top, a volunteer for readiness to be sliced and pickled: a life given without any protest.

In the far corner of the garden, a young peach tree framed the sky and beneath it, a clutch of blue-black feathers refracted, their sheen grabbed my eye and drew me towards it. Here lay a magpie, all feathers and beak and little enamel claws, all teeming with woodlice and fine-winged flies and ants, her once obsidian eyes deep holes that lead to worms with full bellies. I crouched beside her and admired the shape of her long tail and her flashing-blue-ness against the green grass dotted with immature and rotting peach flesh as it moldered into the ground.

JEANNE CASEY

On not wanting.

Quiet now wind. I hear you.
Don't tell me I want. Here
remind me of the joy of feeling
your embrace as sun warms my face.
Stop to forget a moment what was I thinking
Teasel stands stiff and spiny
against wind. Life buzzes by.
Love is the same as if I
was parting the grass with toes
seeds clinging to denim
to this point. This creek teeming
with life. Soil crawling on skin
with billions of microbes.
What if I lay on top of you
allow my blood to mingle
with your skin, feed some microbe.
Were penstemon to grow
from my eye sockets
Would you love me less?

As I want to die,

You are trying to keep me alive, I think.
For why else would you call me out here
again and again to remind me
of ancient beginnings?
You are trying to remind me, I think
again and again all is reborn.
For why else would you have me write
of prairie smoke and note its brown leaves
laying against the ground
from which spindly stalks rise.
I have no choice but to see
Prairie
Mullein
Savior
standing tall stalk sage green
proud from hard line rock crevice.
See you say how it lives
no less strong than that which
is spoiled under your hand
drunk on worm tea.

What, I ask, if I don't want to be reminded
to be nurtured and cradled in waves of grass warmed by the sun?
Would you allow my body to return to where it is comfortable
and forget
the growing hollow
in deep crevices?

KELLY FINE

Through Years and Miles of Sun

Her small mirror is pointed upward. In it, the woman sees a ponderosa branch. She loves ponderosas, loves to bask in their shade, loves to watch their needles gleam with sun like icicles melting away, returning to light. But a mercy of clouds has arrived in the last hour, and the sky in her mirror is a storm-swirled white that makes the pine branch look black. She can feel the thirst of the grass-land surrounding her, and today she would stretch her arms wide to a thunder-storm. The clouds make no promises, the woman feels no more than a healthy breeze, but the pine above her sounds cold in that breeze, like it's wringing snow from June air.

She has sat under this pine many times. Nearly every summer, she camps in full sunlight ten minutes' walk away. She comes to immerse in the prairie with teachers and friends, and also without them. Under this pine, she can find enough solitude to think, to write. It offers just enough shade to let her pupils dilate to a flowing immensity of sky and hills. Trees are few in this land of wildflowers and shin-high bunchgrasses. Though she sits low on a slope, her view of the hills that surround her is vast. Those hills swell and dip with the smoothness of dunes, as if wind were always sweeping and swirling them into place.

Today a good teacher has asked her to point the small mirror upward and focus on its image. The branch in the glass: she wonders why its needles splay apart, exposing their whole bodies to crisping sun, to wind that will gulp water they could use. On a steep slope of low, bending grasses, of small shrubs and forbs wise to drought and wind, how does the pine keep pushing skyward?

Now in the mirror, the woman's face slides in. It's an odd angle to see a face. Back home, her phone sometimes reverses its stare from the insect she's excited to identify and shows her own face nodding at the ground. She says, I look like *that?* and scrambles to return the camera to the bug before it shows her more. But today it isn't a double chin she sees first. She sees a smile she didn't know she was wearing, a smile that radiates the strength of these prairie hills. She sees two braids, sunglasses, and a canvas sun hat whose brim now fills the small mirror, hiding the pine above. She is glad to see the spreading hat, even its dirty chinstrap: the hat means she is out in the sun's world, breathing the pine-litter dust of today.

From this angle, her neck is prominent. She sees its longest scar softening with age. New creases are just beginning to form around the scar, and between them, her skin is raising dots slighter than goosebumps. Decades ago, the first sur-geon said she could die if he left the tumor alone. He said the only thing his blade would steal was her power to put on earrings without a mirror. She was young, and he was an expert. Of course she let him open her neck, her throat.

Now her neck holds a third set of tumors. She can't see them from this angle, but she doesn't mind if people spot the lumps she has chosen to keep carrying. Even the doctors call them benign. The tumors have been with her for eighteen years, and she has slowly come to believe in the power of her wild body to host these living masses and breathe. At home, she lets paper wasps live above her back door. When she first saw them starting a nest, she worried that just turning the doorknob would alarm them. Soon she came to feel that the nest was suffused with a humming peace. The wasps accepted her as part of the home that held them, the good place where they could build cradles and feed their siblings soft caterpillars. Oh, there is one of her masses in the mirror, the mound beneath her ear. It's pulsing lightly with each beat of her heart, innocent as those humming sisters tending to their small tasks.

The woman looks at her mouth in the glass. Her lips have never been pillowy, but when she was younger, her mouth blushed its own red and perched at an angle she hoped was coy. Now her mouth is settling and rolling inward, leaving a shady crevice where her lips meet. The woman sees the deepening furrows that surround her mouth, the wake of more ripples beyond, and she thinks of her younger self, how she would hate this face and hide its lines, turning toward shadows, insisting on candles—

And now the woman is laughing. Her younger self, rigid with seriousness, had so much to learn, so many reasons to look forward. The woman puckers her lips at her reflection and lets go. Pucker lines remain, sharp creases extending halfway to her nose, her chin. The woman did not know the skin around her mouth could now hold memories this way, and the change strikes her as funny. The woman is laughing. The woman is happy. She hasn't spent much time with mirrors lately.

Oh, how she used to worry over mirrors. Once in a while, they said she could pass for a magazine beauty—if only she could live her whole days in just the right angle of lamplight. Mostly, of course, they said she didn't stand a chance. It was all that mirrors talked about, this question; over and over, they called her back for more debate. Not until after her surgeries did the woman begin to believe that the uncontained sun did not hate her. It wasn't that the sun called her perfect or pretty, or that it denied the blades that had mangled her throat for good. No, the sun called her to leave her tiny bedroom, her walled-off mirror. The sun called her to tiptoe into its blaze and, with growing strength, stride out and out beyond.

She is 48 now, and she's seen some sun. Her face once leapt; now it has begun to sag. The earth is calling her downward, and she does not want to die. But she's been coming to this prairie for nine years to sleep within shifting constellations of coyotes and wake to old women unzipping distant tents, old women calling good morning. These women have carried their scars and their laugh lines through years and miles of sun. Here they slip unseen into her tent and leave raptor feathers. Here they stand surrounded by dragonflies and damselflies and butterflies, pointing and whispering names. Their many hands brace her wobbly creek crossings. Sometimes she falls anyway, and many women are there to laugh with her, and if the day is hot, she's thankful all afternoon for shoes that keep bubbling mucky water.

Now a cool wind whooshes the pine above her. All around her body, wind flattens bunchgrasses against the slope. It rolls yarrow and lupine, swirls the canyons of her ears, and pushes upslope, away. She looks down at the mirror in her lap. Her face has slipped out of the picture, and color has returned to the sky, vivid blue between pine needles. Why confine her eyes to the glass? Out in the open, magpies are taunting the wind, and there's time before dinner for a walk.

She zips the mirror into her backpack and clambers down the steep slope, mostly scooting on her butt and palms. At the bottom she brushes off her pants and begins to walk, squinting a little, between the massive bodies of hills. The late afternoon smells like curing grasses and somehow too like the warm webs between her fingers. She hears the hoarse cry of a redtail and looks up to see the hawk flow beyond the crest of a hill. The shadow of a cloud glides the face of the same hill, stroking a swell, now rippling an outcrop. Beside her, the woman's own shadow bumps along over the two-track, its grit and its grasses. Noticing her dark shadow, she grins and turns toward its twin legs, wide sun hat and uneven braids. Her throat will never fully heal, but her shadow looks sturdy and it looks like hers.

She's still standing there gazing at her shadow when something cold taps her elbow. Something cold plinks her wrist. She looks up, and yes—a cloud is letting a few fat drops fall through the sunlight. More rain may come, and she is out in the open. She takes off her hat and tilts back her head. Who knows how long she'll breathe the vast? Today cold raindrops plonk her cheeks. Today her tongue can taste.

ALIDA THACHER

My Previous Life as a Cow Pie

Thumping hooves, skittering
scurries, beating wings.
Whiffs of sweet, musky, stinky, spicy.
Moos, screeches, howls, hoots,

and weather. Lots of weather.
Astonishing arrays of grasses,
many so tenderly delicious
you could graze till the cows

come home. Some grasses
just make you sick. Bessie always
knew the difference. She came
from intelligent stock, grazing

and living long and well
with her cow friends, scattering
cow pies across the prairie.
She pooped me out during

a particularly good season of bunchgrass.
I was fat and flat, a pretty greenish brown
with an extraordinary odor:
Half prairie, half sky.

Droppings, scat, pellets, dung—
words tossed by hikers and bikers,
scientists and scholars,
people who ponder which animal left

what pile of excrement
in the dust. I am
a genus so rare,
I have my own name.

I am *Cow Pie*.
Like treats right out of the oven,
when everyone within smelling distance
comes running to the kitchen.

Like the old bakery on the corner
world famous for its lemon meringue.
Like what you order at the diner at 2 am
to remind you of your mother.

Cow pies are the best.
I lasted longer than Bessie,
long enough to dry out,
stretch wide, get back to the land.

In time, I became a mother myself.
Tiny beings built homes underneath me.
I was their roof, their
protection, their sustenance.

These diverse communities
lasted for generations—
16,000 years
in bug time.

Eventually, I became cracked, dry,
flakey, no nutrition left,
no good at sheltering anymore.
Little beings found younger cow pies.

I wasn't sad. I'd done my part.
Found by two cowpokes, I became
firewood. Cow pies descend
from a long line of firekeepers.

It was my honor to go up in flames.

TOM BUTTS

We Are That Old

I have been here since the beginning.

I rippled and tore the waters
when waters and stones were all that were.

I am that old.

I brought the rains
that eroded the rocks
that rose above the waters
that made these hills and valleys.

I am that old.

I change directions
depending upon my mood.
Today I am feisty and scramble north.

It is I that dance
and fling and flounce
wheatgrasses and fescues.

Snowberry bounces,
shakes and wiggles
in my presence.

Some days I lie down and rest.
I whisper through canyons.
I caress ridges
and kiss your cheeks.

It is I that brings the storm
that brings the rain
that feeds the grasses
that feed the deer
that feed you.

I will be here as long as earth abides.

I will never abandon you
for you and I are one,
eternal,
powerful.

We are that old.

Tom Butts

Listen

Shhhhh. Listen…
When the breeze dancing through wheatgrasses
drops away
to a whisper

You might hear
tinkle of children's laughter,
gossip of women while drying camus root,
neigh of Appaloosa.

You might hear muffled sobbing
on the breeze
as the People leave this prairie
their home
against their will.

You might hear *baaaaing* of sheep,
lowing of cattle
bark of a dog
yip yip of cowboys and cowgirls
moving cattle from summer range
to winter canyons.

Amidst the yodel of meadowlarks
and the chee chee cheree of a sparrow
you might,
if you listen,
hear poetry
spring from this land

Like lupine
Like stone

You might

Tabitha Glaser

Prairie Teachers

The prairie is a testament to
        and a teacher of
                transition.
I want
    to be
        like her.
I was told the dry creek bed would take me
back to camp, and so I went.
Always follow the path of water, she will give you
    what is necessary to carry on.

There is an art to hiking in a dry creek bed: walking in the footsteps of water is no easy task, and requires light feet that can dance across stones.

Flow.

As I'm watching the rocks slide under my feet, I notice one big, white, sun-bleached bone, and then another, a cookie-crumb trail of animal bones leading to a shady spot beneath a tree. Femur, fragments of jaw, and vertebrae that once stacked straight in the spine of a creature fed by the prairie were now cemented in soil, each piece a part of something that once was. Each piece a part of something new, waiting to be.

My body feels drained and dispersed like these bones. My head in one place, my heart in another, a hand extending to grasp something just out of reach, gut wrenching with indecision, while my feet remain rooted in familiarity (or is it fear?). I don't remember how all these parts used to work together as one. It has been so long.

How long have these bones been sitting out here in the sun? How many heat waves, blizzards, and tens of feet of snow have they endured? When the prairie winds were whipping and whispering,

No, not whispering, but shouting,

How could these bones stay still and perfectly untouched?
Do bones grieve the body they have lost?

This I know: the bones belonged to the body of a horse, and the horse's bones lay in a grassy meadow, in a small canyon, where prairie winds rush down the hillside with as much gusto as a roaring waterfall. I wonder if the horse broke a leg here and was mercifully put down underneath the tree by an early pioneer. Or perhaps, the horse escaped from its corral and a wild animal, be it bear or cougar, came down upon it and brought its body to permanent rest here in the cool shade. One body ceremoniously sacrificed for the life of another.

Regardless of its demise, a funeral procession of wild beasts must have ensued postmortem, each visitor taking a small part of the victim to carry with them, either in their bellies or home to their babies. First the flies would come to kiss the body with their long proboscis, almost in apology for its untimely death, but mostly in gratitude for the feast that lay before them and their offspring. Then the scavengers would come from land and air, vultures, coyotes, and the like, to pay respect to another life lost in the prairie. Bigger beasts would come and go, scaring off some funeral attendees, but they would take their piece and be off again. Maggots and grub would not be left out of the party, of course, and would eat some of the less desirable bits of scraps. The horse's skin would puff up and swell at first, only to sag and sink inward with time, slowly decaying in the sweltering heat of the sun. This process would continue on for weeks (months?) until there was nothing left but the bones. Only the bleach-white bones remain after all these years. The structure that once housed a life.

Did this horse know about death? Did it know the offering its body would become?

If the horse was mauled by vicious prey, that's what I feel like. Picked apart before I was fully dead, before the lights went out, before I was able to see my ancestors in the silver lining of the sky. I saw a friend in a foe, and laid down beneath the shade of a solitary tree in a wide-open prairie waiting for him, wanting him to come. At first his nips and licks seemed playful, but bit by bit, he tore me apart with his teeth. I didn't notice it until it was too late, but by then pieces of me were missing and tossed aside out of reach, or completely ingested by the cunning carnivore. I could do nothing but sit and allow myself to be eaten, bit by bit. There was no use in screaming because no one would be able to fix *this*. No one would be able to find me here in *this* place. No one would know how to put my pieces back together. I allowed myself to be consumed.

When we were children and would complain that we were "dying" of heat, or hunger, or exhaustion, my grandmother would respond in German,

> *Es ist hart zu leben; aber härter ist es noch zu sterben.*
> *It is hard to live, but even harder to die.*
> It is hard to transition,
>   transition,
>   transition,
>   only to be met
> with death
>   the final transition.
>   *or is it the final transition?*

In this moment, standing by sunning bones in this wild place where sweet breezes and sunshine constantly kiss my skin, living feels easy. It is *this* present moment that I want to live in forever. I don't want to *transition* anymore. I am scared of the beasts that live back home, and how I will survive what lies ahead. I press on because I must, because I live for moments like *this*. But would it really be harder to die? Would it really be so bad to be bones laid out on the prairie for only the adventurous to discover?

People tell me that when the spring rains arrive to the Prairie and the snow melts, water fills the empty creek bed for a season, bringing life back to the land.

The spark of transition.

The full creek signals the awakening of the prairie, a time of spectacular transformation where plants and animals alike wake up again and start anew in the season of rebirth. Perennials feel the change of soil and sky in their roots and rhizomes, while seeds incubate in the soil, ready for summer. The ground squirrels start to crawl out of their tiny holes, procreate, and store food for slimmer times, constantly chittering at their friends and families. Prairie lizards emerge to sun themselves on rocks, ever on the lookout for predators. Life is not guaranteed here, or anywhere, and yet life is always guaranteed.

The Prairie has always been here, since time immemorial. It has not always looked the same, but the land has always been here bubbling beneath the surface of ancient oceans, shifting under and up against tectonic plates allowing its earth to be molded by prehistoric lava flows, earthquakes, floods, and ice. The Prairie never once said,

"Wait! Stop! I like the way things are! I'm not ready to change!"

The Prairie accepts each transition with grace and a quiet knowing
that life will continue to
pulse on,
    pulse on,
        pulse on.

The transition is not the end.

I walked on, and was wakened from my musings by thousands of tiny blue butterflies leaping up from the yellowing leaves of willow and tall grass. Here was the place where the water from the dry creek bed ran down the rocks and collected in a stagnant pool. The air was thicker here by the water's edge, more humid. Camp was within view, but I was not quite there yet. I was at the final resting place of the spring stream. Here the water would wait patiently to be evaporated into thin air, carried up into the clouds, and then re-dispersed over some vast ocean, or thick jungle, or sprinkled in snow on a mountaintop, or perhaps over another prairie field.

Each drop, a piece of something new waiting to be.

Here I am: a piece of something new wanting to be.
I am ready to transcend into some ethereal cloud
above the Prairie and begin anew.

House of Sky—CMarie Fuhrman

THANK YOU

While our days were filled with walking and writing, with tuning into the sounds and silences of all Beings on the Zumwalt Prairie, without the grace and sustained presence of every person in late June of 2024, there would not be this beautiful anthology before you.

Thank you first to the organizations that make the Summer Outpost possible, including Fishtrap and The Nature Conservancy, who allow us to be on the land and return to Summer Camp each year. And to those people who worked behind the scenes: Fishtrap's program director Mike Midlo, who pulled the organizational strings; The Nature Conservancy's Jeff Fields, who shared insights into what it takes to manage the Zumwalt Prairie Preserve, and the Outpost Summer Camp's caretakers Jeff Osmundson and Colleen Shannon, who witnessed our gathering and took the *Howl* photo on the back cover of this anthology.

Just as our hearts were filled with the sounds of the Zumwalt—coyotes at night, wind rustling the bunchgrass—without the amazing meals Outpost cooks Kelsey Juve and Becca Pulcranno served up three times each day, none of us would have thrived. Gratitude for these meals. They allowed us to break bread with new friends. May those friendships sustain us for many years.

And even if not every participant contributed a piece of writing or art, they are here in these pages as well, their voices whispering between the lines. So, thank you to Devon Van Essen and Jolene Tucker for your presence at Zumwalt.

Our kind thanks to Janet Hohmann, biologist and naturalist, who helped illuminate the prairie-scapes, wildflowers, herds of elk, and all other beings on the prairie. What a wonderful guide to our presence and our writing on the prairie.

We who camped out, ate together, walked together, and wrote and wrote and wrote, would not have tapped into our bodies as part of that beautiful land and all its beings—past, present and future—without the guidance and kindness of CMarie Fuhrman. We were told by her that we had a right to be there. The lenses we acquired from CMarie will sustain us into the future. For that there are not enough words to say thank you.

Thanks to Western Colorado University and Blue Feathered Quill for bringing this to press.

We believe that each of us came to "read" some pages of the Prairie, and that we took those lessons back to our home places. Our words may be a poor substitute for the experience of being on that eastern Oregon prairie, but, dear reader, we hope this anthology comes close to taking you there.

Your editors,
Francis Opila, Tom Butts, and Connie Wieneke
Wallowa County, Oregon, 2024

Zumwalt Outpost Bio Sketches

Tom Butts is a professional wildlife biologist who has studied everything from bighorn sheep to bats, mostly in the western U.S. but as far afield as Ghana. He has spent most of his life in the upper Missouri River watershed but has been fortunate to have traveled far and wide. Now and again he enjoys putting pen to paper.

Jeanne Casey is a writer in Portland, OR. When not writing, she enjoys working in her garden, hiking with her dog and husband, and hanging out with her chickens. Jeanne is convinced she is not a writer of poetry despite evidence to the contrary.

Carol Dodds came into this experience to find out if it is worthwhile to write and found a wonderful new family whose support she cherishes and whose work she relishes. This is the first time her work is in print.

Amelia Díaz Ettinger is a Mexican-born, Puerto Rican-raised teacher, biologist, poet, and writer. She is the proud mother of two amazing human beings and four brand new souls in this world that she calls her grandkids. Besides being the matriarch of this brood, she loves mountain biking, knitting, quilting, and chilling in her corner of the world in Eastern Oregon with family, friends, and nature.

Kelly Fine treasures the community of earth writers that she has found in eleven years of Outpost and Summer Fishtrap workshops. A few years ago, she moved to Austin, Texas, a city on the border between her beloved West and the green lands beyond—but distance cannot keep her from Wallowa County. Contact her at *kellykinneyfine@gmail.com.*

Tabitha Glaser has had her hand in many occupations from farmer to caregiver to teacher, but she has always been a writer at heart. Despite drafting many stories since second grade, this is her first piece in print. She lives with her two daughters and a mini-Australian shepherd named Gypsy in the Willamette Valley at a place where the railroad tracks and the Santiam River cross paths.

At the Zumwalt Outpost **Francis Opila** was given the Red-tailed Hawk oracle card. On the first morning he was rewarded with his trip bird—the Ferruginous Hawk. His poetry collection *Conference of the Crows* was published in 2023. He enjoys performing poetry, combining recitation and playing North American wooden flutes. *https://francisopila.com/.*

Alida Thacher has explored many roles as an author, producer, and teacher. The stars say she is a truthteller, a seeker, a student, a sage, an optimist, a philosopher; that's as good a description as any. She is fascinated by robots and A.I., but she always writes her first drafts by hand.

Janie Tippett is a longtime Fishtrapper, rancher, writer, mother, grand, great and now great great grandmother, historian, gardener, and hunting camp cook. She has published 7 books, has been published in numerous anthologies and wrote a newspaper column for 31 years. She celebrated her 91st birthday in September 2024.

Since 1983 **Connie Wieneke** has lived in Wyoming. All of her writing is fueled by place and family, by the ways in which memory sometimes gets it wrong. At Zumwalt the cards she drew were killdeer and dragonfly. Seemed fitting. Links to her work can be found on *blackhen.com*.

Rebecca Williams is a current MFA student at Western Colorado University. She lives in Atlanta with her family and a collection of beasts.